The Miracles of God

Life With Down Syndrome

By Rosie Mullen

The Miracles of God

Life with Down syndrome

By Rosie Mullen

The Miracles of God

Rosie Mullen

G & R Publishing

Birmingham, AL

All Scripture references contained herein are quoted from the New King James Version of the Holy Bible.

Library of Congress Cataloging-in-Publication Data

Library of Congress Control Number: 2015938883

Mullen, Rosie

The Miracles of God

    I. Religious. 2. Christian.

ISBN: 978-0-578-15895-2

Table of Contents

Dedication

This book is dedicated to my wonderful husband Greg who stayed by my side through this tedious experience, to our four older children LaSondra, Greg Jr., Genesis and Trinity for their patience and understanding through this whole experience. To my sister Bessie who has been so inspirational with her words of encouragement. It is also dedicated to my spiritual daughters Betty Jackson and Felecia Mitchell who have been there with me daily. To our parents and siblings for their continued support, to my entire family at Nest of Love Christian Church for standing by us and showing an enormous amount of love and to Brenda Lovelady Spahn for giving a positive outlook, spiritual wisdom and direction at such a needed time. We thank God for putting the right people in our lives, in the right place and at the right time.

Introduction

Dear Reader,

As I sat down to begin the writing of this book, I wanted to take the time to share with you the reason for my writing. As I write, I have so many people in mind and I hope that as I share my story, each and every one can find themselves within the pages of what I believe to be is God's grand design.

This book is for the pregnant woman who never expected to be pregnant again. This book is for the young mother who never expected this to happen to her because she thought it only happened to older mothers. This book is for the mother's and families who have been entrusted with a child who has Down syndrome. This book is for the child themselves who is diagnosed, who need to be reminded that each one of them are one of God's miracles. This book is for the woman, man and believer who, whether it is physical, emotional or spiritual, needs reassurance that God is in control and has their best interests at heart.

As you read the story of my Miracle, I sincerely hope that you can see the hand of God along every step of the way. After I became pregnant, I would very quickly find that for the first time, I needed God in a way that I had never experienced before. I was broken and needed many, many miracles. I had become so accustom to sharing God with others during their time of need, but now found myself in my own dilemma.

My prayer is that the purpose and ministry contained in these pages are very clear. I hope that as I tell my story, it is evident that without God, I truly never could have made it through my pregnancy, through the life that I now live with little Miracle or through the spiritual lessons that God has brought my way. When I needed Him the most, He was right there and still continues to be there.

If you get nothing else out of what you read in these pages, there are three connected things that I pray you walk away believing:

1. God has a plan to prosper you. Trust in that fact when you don't seem to understand where you are.
2. God will provide miracles along each step of the way if you would trust and believe in His plan.
3. Even when you can't seem to hear His voice, trust His plan.

Blessings to you,

Rosie Mullen

Chapter 1

If It Was Not For God...

For I know the thoughts that I think toward you, saith the Lord, thoughts of peace, and not of evil, to give you an expected end.

Jeremiah 29:11

On August 4, 2008, my life changed forever. I remember it clearly: It was a beautiful day filled with sunshine, hot, and without a cloud in the sky. I had just begun a Daniel's fast but this time, I didn't feel well physically and I didn't feel like I could do it. Normally when I did a Daniel's fast I did feel weak and famished, but this time it was harder than ever before. Due to how I felt physically it began to weigh on me mentally and spiritually. It started to take a toll on me and it was difficult for me figure out what was going on. I started to think; maybe it is because I am getting older.

I was forty two years old. I knew that my body was changing and I began to think that menopause was slowly creeping upon me. I had recently begun teaching my women's group at church about the effects of menopause. I was feeling a change at this point in my life and was experiencing hot flashes, fatigue and nausea. I had been reading up on menopause so I knew the symptoms consisted of mood swings. So I really thought I was prepared and I wanted to make sure that our women's group was prepared also. I also knew that irregular cycles were one of the symptoms of menopause. However, I had a flash go through my mind because my cycle the previous month had been irregular. So I decided to teach more thoroughly and explain how menopause usually starts and what symptoms to expect. At this juncture of my life I knew that my body transforming from the body of a young woman to that of a middle-aged woman. I was having mood swings, cold sweats, and a few more cramps than normal. I really thought I knew what was going on with my body. The symptoms continued and I truly did not feel good. This went on for several days; my sense of smell awakened. Greg and I became concerned because we both knew that with my last four pregnancies my sense of smell was very active. After laughing at what we thought surely was not the case, we decided that I should take a pregnancy test. I now believe that this was how God was ordering my steps and revealing His plan. Rather than going to the doctor we went to the drug store and purchased a home pregnancy test.

As we walked through this process and took this test together, we found out that God truly did have a plan that most certainly, I was pregnant. After finding out this news, Greg and I felt like Abraham and Sarah. Here I was, a forty two year old woman with four children and I was going to be a mother again. Physically, I had been through so much while carrying my other four children. From Fibroids to a drooping bladder, and a stretched uterus, I thought my childbearing days were over. This was certainly a rude awakening. I was horribly sick during pregnancy with all of my children and I wasn't looking forward to that again. My husband sat with me in the bathroom in shock and in awe as I shared the news. But as he and I would be reminded again and again over the days to come, God has plans for us all. We looked at each other and came to the conclusion God truly does have a sense of humor.

Deciding to share this news with the children, they all actually thought that mom being pregnant was funny. Greg and I dreaded telling them because they were all at the age where they understood the process of how babies are born. We dreaded it mainly because all of them, except one, were at an age where they understood where babies came from.

So, when we shared the news with them, they all fell out on the floor laughing obnoxiously. They thought that we were joking about being pregnant. I am so glad that God gave us grace even in those moments.

As we journeyed into this unexpected pregnancy, the first twelve weeks were unlike any of my other pregnancies. It was the best experience I ever had as a pregnant woman. This is the time that I knew God was with me. I experienced such a peace and assurance. I felt like Peter; I stepped out on the waters with my focus on the triune God. I did not get sick like with my other children and it was a happy and joyous time. It was a time where I was truly able to believe that God was in complete control and undoubtedly involved in this pregnancy because Greg and I had nothing to do with it. It makes me think of a passage of Scripture that talk about time.

But when the fullness of the time had come, God sent forth His Son, born[a] of a woman, born under the law, to redeem those who were under the law, that we might receive the adoption as sons.

Galatians 4:4-5

The baby inside of me was no Jesus Christ, but this scripture reminds me that all great things and all great miracles happen in God's time. Reader, if there is one thing that I want to impress upon you about what God showed me during this genesis of my miracle's life, it is that you have to trust in God's plan even when it is not your own. I was not expecting to get pregnant and to be honest, was not planning it. I could have stepped out of the will of God by pushing away the blessing He was bringing my way. But because I was willing to submit to His will, blessings came my way and provision began to flow. The same can happen for the situation that God has ordained for you.

Very soon, I would be entering into a time when I would need a mighty move of God. I would soon need Him to intervene on my behalf. I would soon be taught that God's plan sometimes includes periods of testing and trial. But for now, I understood that this was a time and a child that was ordained by God and I was thankful for it all.

Chapter 2

A Shift

My second trimester marked the beginning of a change in my pregnancy. I was called to minister at our two day *Breaking Free* women's conference. During the conference, I witnessed God move mightily on behalf of the women. So many ladies were dealing with depression, infertility, brokenness and deep hurt. I was able to lay hands, pray, intercede on their behalf and see God bring them out of darkness. It was a time that was so precious and divinely ordained.

I preached, prayed and ministered my heart out at this conference. It was like the word of God in Isaiah 61:1 came to life through me.

"The Spirit of the Lord God is upon Me,

Because the Lord has anointed Me

To preach good tidings to the poor;

He has sent Me to heal the brokenhearted,

To proclaim liberty to the captives,

And the opening of the prison to those who are
bound"

The Holy Spirit used me in a mighty way on that night on behalf of those women. This was one of the highest points of divine connection that I have ever had in ministry.

Not only was this was one of the most amazing women's conferences that I have ever been a part of but it was one of the most amazing that I have ever attended. The atmosphere was electric; the Spirit of God was phenomenal. It was as if you could touch the hem of His garment in that room. God allowed me to bring a bag of rocks as part of the message for that night. I had labeled these rocks as "Bitterness", "Depression", "Addiction", "Lust", Bad Habits", etc. These were attached to me in a bag connected to my jacket. So I walked into that conference demonstrating how women are secretly carrying luggage and baggage that are many times unseen to the world around them. I preached about how we needed to release our baggage, the things that are hidden on the inside and that we need to release it and let it go. The longer we hold on to it the more difficult it becomes to let it go and we remain in bondage. Eventually we will become accustomed to the bondage and will not realize that we can "Break Free".

God allowed me to break free from many of those strongholds and barriers and through my deliverance I was able to help other women to break free also. We were all carrying loads that were keeping us in bondage and I was admonishing the women to let go of the things that were holding them back.

God was revealing things that the women were dealing with and were hiding. On that night, God called them to the surface and set free many souls. There was truly a spirit of liberation in that room.

Very soon, there would be a shift in my own life. I preached freedom in that conference and very soon, would find myself at the very altar of God.

Three days later, I truly began to travail. I became one of those women. I started having contractions like never before. I was experiencing pains that I had not felt in my previous pregnancies. These contractions were unlike anything I had ever experienced; they were even more painful than actually giving birth.

The contractions gave way to hemorrhaging and on that third night I was admitted to the hospital. I was threatening to have a miscarriage. I was now that woman in pain who was crying out and needing a mighty move of God.

This was the beginning of the time when God began to do a new, painful thing in me. Lying in that hospital bed with blood streaming out of my body in waves and bursts, I could not help but to ask God why He was allowing this to happen. I was crying out to him in pain and in confusion. I was afraid and I was hurting. The blood clots were the size of soft balls and very quickly, the doctors became concerned for both the baby's life and my own.

This situation was so ironic because I had never been in a situation where I was in so much need. Being in ministry and always being the person to pour into others, I had never really experienced what it felt like to need a miraculous move of God in my own life. I had been the avenue that God had used at the conference for those women in need and in the past, I had been used in the spiritual lives of those at church. Now, I needed God in my life like never before. I was experiencing something totally new and had reached a place in my life that I had never been. It was one thing to see other women there and be that person that helped walk with them and pray with them in their situation. But now I found myself in the same position as they were and this woman of God was definitely in need of a miracle.

When the doctor came in, I could see the fear on his face. He let me know that he could not let me continue to bleed the way I was. He told me that my life was in danger. When I saw the look on his face it made me realize how serious this was. I reached out and grabbed my husband's hand and he began to pray.

The only thing that doctor could tell me to do was to lie as still as possible for the rest of the night. He would then check on me every half hour until he and his team could determine what direction they needed to take.

I knew right then that if God did not move on my behalf; I could lose my life and the life of my child.

While I was lying as still as possible, the Lord sent me a word. I know now that it was a word that would save my life and speak directly to my situation.

"And Moses said to the people, "Do not be afraid. Stand still, and see the salvation of the Lord, which He will accomplish for you today."

Exodus 14:13 was the verse that saved my life. I became still and began expecting a move of God. My husband, who was by my side the entire time, began to read the words of Scripture over me as he sat in the chair beside my bed. My friend who has been my prayer partner over the years was also there. She began to pray as well. She must have prayed for two hours straight without ceasing. Slowly and surely, even though I continued to bleed, my faith began to be renewed. I experienced a deeper sense of peace and assurance in the Lord as I allowed Him to take control of the situation. I began to believe and trust that He was in control and that whatever came my way, I was in His will and He had a plan for me, even in this. I began to feel refreshed and I got excited because I felt sure that God was going to work this out. I was so excited it was difficult to just lay still.

That night was one of the most spiritually rich nights that I have ever experienced. It was historical. Slowly, the hemorrhaging lessened and by midnight it had stopped. I did not know that a person could lose as much blood as I had lost and still live.

The next morning, the doctors were prepared to perform the DNC procedure. They expected to see a lifeless baby in my womb and were prepared to remove it from me. Fortunately, my doctor decided to do an ultrasound before the procedure and when he did so, he found the baby tucked up under the right side of my ribcage. It was such an amazing sight to see. It was as she was looking directly into the camera as they took the picture with the ultrasonic camera. She didn't appear to be hanging on for dear life but rather seemed to display an indication of confidence.

Her heartbeat was so strong. The doctors and nurses couldn't believe that she was still hanging in there after all of the blood that I had lost. What amazed me is that when I spoke to him, the doctor said "I wish I could say that it was something that I had done but I cannot. It had to be divine intervention."

Immediately I knew that God had worked a miracle on my behalf.

From a night of losing so much blood and communing with God deeply in prayer, this morning opened up to a brand new miraculous day. The entire atmosphere in the room changed from one of crying out and despair to one of praise and worship and adoration for my God. I was experiencing a joy that I had never experienced before. It was due to the fact that God had heard our prayers and answered our petitions. At my weakest moment God had moved and I was now experiencing a joy on the inside that turned into strength on the outside. Later that day, I was able to find the energy to get up and walk out of that hospital still pregnant and hopeful.

That morning, my husband and I knew what we would name this baby. We could do nothing but to name her Miracle.

That morning, I was reminded of the story of the woman with the issue of blood. To bleed for twelve years and then to be healed by God through faith, I knew that she was a miracle. I felt like her sister. I knew that God had kept me through that night and I knew that he would continue to keep me. I took the next two weeks off of work but I worked from home as an accountant.

After those two weeks, I went back to work and life continued on. I was a walking, breathing, baby-carrying miracle of God. I felt good and had no other complications. At my next doctor's visit, we were able to confirm that the baby was healthy and growing. We also learned that she was a girl. I was still pregnant with my Miracle.

Chapter 3

The Calm Before the Storm

The next five months were a whirlwind of positivity. I was feeling good and felt like God had gotten us through a major storm in our lives. At this point, I was not only amazed at what God had done in saving both my own and Miracle's lives, but I was shocked at how he managed to bless us in ways beyond comprehension.

I was still working full time at a transitional facility for women but also had the responsibility of maintaining my health and raising my other children. I was also still teaching and preaching at our church who was our other family that I loved and had the responsibility of being the first lady that they needed me to be. Also, I had a husband that I adored and was called to love and minister too. During the time of my sickness, he went through so many emotions, often wondering if he was going to lose his wife and the mother of his children. In all that God had brought me through, I was still being used for His glory to preach, pray and to raise and love so many people. Even when I needed Him most, He was still gracious enough to use me to touch the lives of others.

I also felt great physically. Miracle was a very active baby and as I began to grow and get bigger, she became more and more active. Greg and I marveled by watching my belly move the way it did. It was truly something special. She was more active than any of my other pregnancies.

I received constant monitoring by my doctor. Even though I was fully dependent on the grace and hand of God, I was also thankful for the doctors that he sent to care for me. They were very thorough and caring.

My doctor suggested that I do some more testing on the baby, tests that looked for Down syndrome and other diagnoses. When we asked him whether or not it was necessary, he responded no. So we did not go through with the testing. To be honest, we did not really care. We were just thankful for the life God had entrusted us with and wanted nothing but to walk in His will and His plan. We felt like we were ready to tackle anything that came our way.

It is funny how our timing is often not God's timing. Very soon, we would learn this up close and personal.

On February 28th, 2009, our friends and family had planned a baby shower on our behalf. I was due to deliver Miracle on March 15th but on the morning of the shower, we woke up to a beautiful day, full of sunshine and blue sky. I was feeling wonderful and as Greg and I lay in bed that morning, we could not help but dwell on how good and faithful God had been toward us. As I lay in Greg's arms, I had a joy and a peace that I would not have given up for anything in the world. We talked about the baby shower planned for later that day and we were so thankful for all that God had provided.

At some point, we decided to get up and get ready for the day ahead. When I stood up, I felt a major physical shift in my belly. It was as if the baby had dropped. Immediately, contractions began very quickly. I immediately felt the physical pain that goes along with being in labor. Very soon afterward, my water broke and I felt the wetness begin to run down my legs.

Miracle was on her way. We would be welcoming her into the world in God's timing and not our own.

With thoughts of the impending baby shower leaving our minds, we immediately got ready to go to the hospital. We were dealing with God's timing and as I think back on it now, so many scriptures come to mind that deal with being dependent on His plan and His time.

And Sarah conceived and bore Abraham a son in his old age at the time of which God had spoken to him (Genesis 21:2 ESV).

My times are in your hand...

(Psalm 31:15 ESV)

For we are his workmanship, created in Christ Jesus for good works, which God prepared beforehand, that we should walk in them

(Ephesians 2:10)

God was sending us our Miracle and we were ready to help bring her into the world.

By the time we got to the hospital, I was already six cm dilated. We arrived just in time for me to be able to receive an epidural. More than anything, experiencing the hand of God in this way made clear the fact that we all are dependent on His time and purpose. He truly is an on time God.

Chapter 4

5 Days in the Whale

Now the Lord had prepared a great fish to swallow Jonah. And Jonah was in the belly of the fish three days and three nights.

Jonah 1:17

Day 1.

The birth of my Miracle was unlike any of my other children. I pushed three times and she was born. The nurses laid her immediately in my arms. She was the most beautiful sight I had ever seen. She was so tiny and so frail. It was like my heart had stopped and I was holding my breath because of the depth of love I was feeling. Miracle was also holding hers.

She was not breathing and was not making a sound. When the nurses noticed this, they immediately took her out of my arms and began to pat her on the back, trying to get her to breathe. She started on her own but in those few moments, as my fear began to build; I knew that this little creature was going to be a very, very special child. She was a miracle.

No more than ten minutes after her birth, Miracle was taken from me. One minute she was there in the room with me and the next, they were rushing her to ICU. The doctor stood next to my bedside and shared words with me that I was not prepared to hear.

The doctor told me that he was not sure, but Miracle had signs of being a child with Down syndrome.

He said that because Miracle had features that look like those of Down syndrome babies and the fact that she stopped breathing almost immediately upon birth, they suspected this diagnosis.

I felt like I couldn't breathe. I did not know why this was happening. I was scared and confused and all I wanted was for my daughter to be healthy and in my arms. The way it was looking, she was neither. One thing I did know was that anytime a miracle happens or when God begins to do something new and special in the lives of His people, the enemy gets mad and tries to do whatever he can to confound the situation.

In many ways, it was like the birth of Moses. When he was born, the Pharaoh ordered all male children two years and younger in the Hebrew nation to be killed because he believed that the Hebrews were becoming too large in number and might overthrow Egypt. Moses however a very special man, the deliverer that God was sending. We know that the story is a victorious one and that Moses' life were divinely protected, but that did not stop the enemy (in that case, Pharoah) from attempting to kill him anyway.

Now, Miracle is no Moses. But she is special. And I believed that the enemy, that crafty and conniving Devil, was trying to snuff her out.

Like any mother would do, I immediately began to pray. Here I was, with a new daughter named Miracle and yet I was in need of another miracle from God. I wanted and needed Him to move supernaturally. I was praying that the doctors would come back and that their diagnosis would be wrong. I felt like Jonah in the belly of the whale; wrapped in seaweed with no way out.

After all the doctors looking at her and making their diagnoses, my little girl was placed in ICU. She could not breathe on her own; oxygen was bypassing her lungs. It was as if her body believed that she was still in the womb and had not been born yet. She could not be held or even touched.

This by far was the longest day of my life. I had just had a baby that I could not interact with physically in any way. Knowing that she was being placed into an incubator with tubes and attachments on her body was heart wrenching. I could not even look at her. The doctors said that light could cause her body more stress than necessary and because of that, they needed to place a blanket over her incubator.

I was in one of the darkest places I have ever been in spiritually. I was believing God for healing and restoration but was still broken, sad and in pain. My husband gave the family the news about what was going on.

Calls started to pour in. Some of them were good ones and some, not so good. Some people were critical and lacked encouragement. We were so tired and drained and in a spiritual upheaval that Greg requested that no visitors come by that day. My other children came to the hospital that night and we cried and prayed and sought the Lord as a family. We made one visit to the ICU as a unit and were only able to have a quick peek into the incubator.

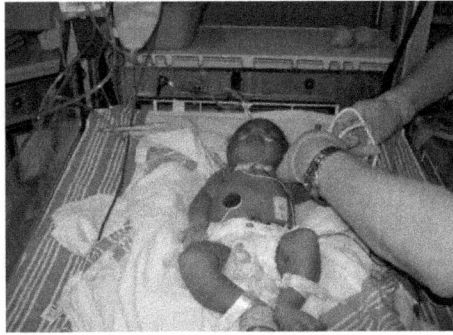

In life, if I had ever thought that I had gone wrong somewhere, that night, I did. I laid down that night and cried myself to sleep hoping that this day and this news had only been a dream.

Day 2.

I woke up the next morning realizing that all of this was not a dream. It was reality.

It was a Sunday morning. Greg had to leave me and prepare to preach at church. His pastoral duties still called. It was a cold and dreary morning and after Greg left, I got dressed, grabbed my bible and forced my way into ICU. It was not visiting hours yet but all I wanted was to be near my baby girl. I was so full of anxiety.

I asked the nurses if I could read the Word over the incubator and they said yes but that I must do it very, very quietly. I sat on a stool in front of her incubator and as I looked out the window, I saw that it was snowing. The flakes were so huge. I realized as I saw the weather transition to blizzard status that I too was in a stage of transition. When I came in on Saturday the sun was shining and now, we were in the middle of a snowstorm. Birmingham had no time to prepare for this.

My excitement was so high yesterday. And now, here I am praying and hoping that my child's vitals would go up so that she could breathe on her own. All I wanted was for her to be healthy enough for me to touch and hold her.

I read the Word to her. It was all that I knew to do. Even in doing so, I was feeling the energy drain from my body so I eventually went back to my room. I was in a dark place. Greg and the kids made it back in time before the roads were shut down.

Day 3

On the third day of being in the hospital, a shift began to happen. While I was still lost and seeking the Lord, doing everything I knew to do in order to find some relief from the pain I was in, Miracle began to interact with the world.

On her own, my child's breathing began to stabilize. While she was not breathing on her own just yet, she began breathing with assisted oxygen in lesser and lesser amounts. Basically, her lungs began to function on their own at 10 percent capacity and upward from there. I touched my child and held her for the first time today. Although only for a short time, with all of the tubes and devices attached to her, I was able to connect with my daughter.

Day 4

The fourth day in the hospital was more of the same. I was in the belly of the whale. I was feeling at fault for what my child was going through and wondering what it was that I had done wrong. I was distraught, in pain, ashamed and feeling disheartened. I continued to pray but felt as if my prayers were bouncing off of the walls of that whale's belly. I related to Jonah's prayer so much.

And he said:

"I cried out to the Lord because of my affliction,
And He answered me.

"Out of the belly of Sheol I cried,
And You heard my voice.

For You cast me into the deep,

Into the heart of the seas,

And the floods surrounded me;

All Your billows and Your waves passed over me.

Then I said, 'I have been cast out of Your sight;

Yet I will look again toward Your holy temple.'

The waters surrounded me, even to my soul;

The deep closed around me;

Weeds were wrapped around my head.

I went down to the moorings of the mountains;

The earth with its bars closed behind me forever;

Yet You have brought up my life from the pit,

O Lord, my God.

"When my soul fainted within me,

I remembered the Lord;

And my prayer went up to You,

Into Your holy temple.

"Those who regard worthless idols

Forsake their own Mercy.

But I will sacrifice to You
With the voice of thanksgiving;
I will pay what I have vowed.
Salvation is of the Lord."

So the Lord spoke to the fish, and it vomited Jonah onto dry land.

Little did I know, I was about to be vomited onto dry land.

Day 5

On day five, my world came to a climax.

I had gone into the ICU to see Miracle and to talk to the nurses. Miracle's doctor was present and without any tact or sense of comfort, he blurted out that, "She's Down. These babies are 'retarded.'"

The diagnosis was official. Before this, the staff only inferred that Miracle had features "similar" to that of a child with Down syndrome. At that point nothing had been confirmed. I had been praying over the last five days that I wouldn't get this news and that the diagnosis was not true. Now, I knew that it was.

I was shocked at the doctor's way of revealing this delicate information. I did not confront the doctor at all but ran out of the ICU. I found it difficult to breathe. Almost hyperventilating, I escaped into my room and fell into a near state of shock.

It was like the world was crashing down around me. God had given me my answer and right now, in this moment, I was not prepared to accept it. It hurt and felt like I was being blamed, condemned or found guilty for something. I did not know what to do.

I found myself on the floor of the bathroom completely in shock. I was not able to respond to anybody or feel anything and I really did not comprehend what was going on around me. Greg had to come into the bathroom and pick me up.

Someone came in to explain to me in detail about Miracle's condition but I was unable to respond at all. I did not move or speak until several hours later when a frantic call came in from a church member who had heard that I died. She was hysterical. She had to pull to the side of the road while driving and would not move until she heard from Greg to know whether it was true or not. Greg had reassured her that I had not passed and that everything was alright.

Prior to this, I was lying there like a vegetable. I was almost lifeless.

I was very close to this person and we had a spiritual bond. To hear that she was distraught helped me to come around. The church member called Greg having been misinformed. It was at the very moment when I heard Greg reassuring this friend that I knew that I had to get up and move. I did not want my friend to believe that she had lost her first lady and prayer partner. I knew that God was working because I found the power to move forward.

I then knew that it had to be God's action. There was no reason why anybody would have said I died. It was this phone call of love and support from our church that broke me out of my state of shock. I was given motivation and the desire and to communicate again.

Like Jonah, I was not prepared to face the reality of the life ahead of me and ahead of Miracle until I had gone through my experience of being in that whale's belly. Thinking back on it, I didn't really start praying the way that God wanted me to pray until I was in there.

When I woke up out of the state of shock I was in, I realized that I had to go on. I not only had to be a rock and support for all that Miracle would need in the upcoming days and years of her life, but to also go on for myself. I had to continue being the woman of God my Lord had called me to be. I had to continue to be a mother and a wife and servant of the Most High God. I had to go on. I had to be like King David when he lost his son. After all of the praying and fasting and crying out to the Lord, I had to wash my face, anoint my head and go on in the power of His might. I could not quit.

This was a miracle in its own right. God had seen me through the darkest of places and I had come out on the other side ready to serve Him all the more.

Chapter 5

Life after Death

The rest of the time in the hospital was amazing. It was like God was proving to me daily that He had a plan and a purpose for every moment that we were there.

Miracle was an amazing baby. Every day, she was making strides and the doctors could not believe that she was developing the way that she was. For a child with Down syndrome, she was exceeding their expectations every day and was blowing their minds. As she grew and developed and reached her milestones, I saw more and more of the hand of God at work.

The only way that I can describe the time after my five days in the belly of the whale is like this:

But now, O LORD, thou art our father; we are the
clay, and thou our potter; and we all are the work of
thy hand.

Jeremiah 64:8

God was not only molding, making and strengthening Miracle's little body, but He was also working on and putting me back together. It was as if He was concerned with my own spiritual life while He was doing work in Miracle as well. I had gone from being a broken, distraught, emotional mess to a woman who was being renewed daily. Now, there were times when I was still in doubt and worried and wanted to know more, but I was nowhere near being the mess that I was a few days before. He was teaching me to be strong in the power of His might.

So many events occurred during the days that Miracle was in the hospital.

On day six, I was able to take Miracle out of the incubator and hold her. It was only for a few minutes because of all of the wires and tubes connected to her. It was a miracle in and of itself that I was able to do so at that particular time.

On the seventh day, Miracle latched onto my breast. Not many people know this, but it is rare for children with Down syndrome to latch on so soon. They usually find it hard to suck because of the low muscle tone in their mouths. However, Miracle was latching on by the seventh day of her life. The doctors were amazed at her developmental progress after she had such difficulty stabilizing her breathing in the incubator. As I watched her meet milestones and astound the doctors and nurses, I began to accept the diagnosis. My faith began to grow. My motherly instinct kicked in and I began to press forward in my faith and in my role as a parent.

On the eighth day, we went to see Mrs. Bell from the Bell Center. She is an amazing woman and a gift from God to my family and I. As we walked in the door of the center and sat down, Mrs. Bell looked me square in the eye and explained that the limits that I would put on Miracle were the only ones that would hinder her. I should expect her to do everything any other baby could do, just at a slower pace. She even told me that the baby that God had given me was a Miracle and she said this without having known any of my background. "I want you to know how special she is she said. Even when some others were not, Mrs. Bell stayed positive. As soon as Miracle came out of the hospital, going to the Bell Center was pivotal in providing insight into families with Down's syndrome, providing physical therapy and everything necessary for Miracle's development. The reading material that Mrs. Bell gave me was all positive and it gave me hope when I thought I had none.

On the ninth day, my sister came and stayed at the hospital with me. She prayed with me and slept in the hospital chair. Her support was amazing; she shared with me about her first baby who also was a miracle, weighing in at only 2 pounds at birth. This was during some of the hard days. She will never know how much of a blessing that this was to me because at the same time, some other friends and family were speaking defeat into my life and were very negative. Just being there for me and praying and reading the word was more than I can ever be grateful for.

Greg too, was such an amazing blessing during this time. Now remember, he is the Pastor of our church and has a congregation to care for. But even with all of his responsibilities, he stayed at the hospital with me every night. And not only was he at the hospital, he took care of our other children and brought them to the hospital as well. The older children did not need much tending to but the younger ones were well taken care of by my husband in those early days. He fed them when necessary and made sure that they were at the hospital to witness Miracle's milestones.

I was really blessed to have my family there in the hospital every night. The hospital gave us a special room where we could eat together. We had the opportunity to do homework, to watch Miracle grow and to be involved in the early needs that she had. We prayed for Miracle as she struggled in the ICU to latch on to life. We sung hymns, read the Word and did everything that we knew how to do. Looking back on it now, I can also see that we were growing closer to God in our own relationships as we rallied around each other in order to support Miracle. Watching my children come together in unity in support of their sister did more for my spirit than can ever be expressed.

I may sound like one of those parents that gloat on the achievements of their child but to be honest, I like it that way. The doctors were truly astonished at how fast Miracle was coming along. Watching them stand in amazement at the hand of God gave me pure joy and it produced within me a song of worship to my Lord. I was not only proud of Miracle but was amazed at God. He truly is the God of miracles.

Children with Down syndrome can have a lot of trouble breathing by themselves. But on the 14th day, Miracle started breathing on her own. The doctors and nurses would take her off of the oxygen for a few minutes at a time and then eventually, they took her off for hours. Her lungs were beginning to develop and strengthen on their own and she was functioning for the first time as if she was truly in the world.

On day fifteen, Miracle went six hours without assisted oxygen. Her oxygen levels were beginning to stabilize and it was wonderful knowing that she was breathing and getting the oxygen she needed.

On day sixteen, Miracle's breathing had stabilized after being off of oxygen for twenty four hours. Then Miracle was allowed to go home without a respirator. What an exciting day that was.

I cannot reiterate enough how much I stand amazed at God during our time in the hospital. I went from a broken, distressed, hysterical mother to a mother who was able to stand in the face of a dire diagnosis and declare that God was still good. I became a woman who knew pain and was still willing to trust in the sovereignty and power of the Almighty. Aside from my miracle child, I was a woman who had seen miracles in their own right. God had not only *given* me a miracle, He had *performed* a miracle in me.

After seeing such a mighty move of God, I was truly able to live again. After experiencing the breath of Jesus, I had truly seen and experienced life after death.

To the only wise God our Saviour, be glory and majesty, dominion and power, both now and ever. Amen.

Jude 1:25

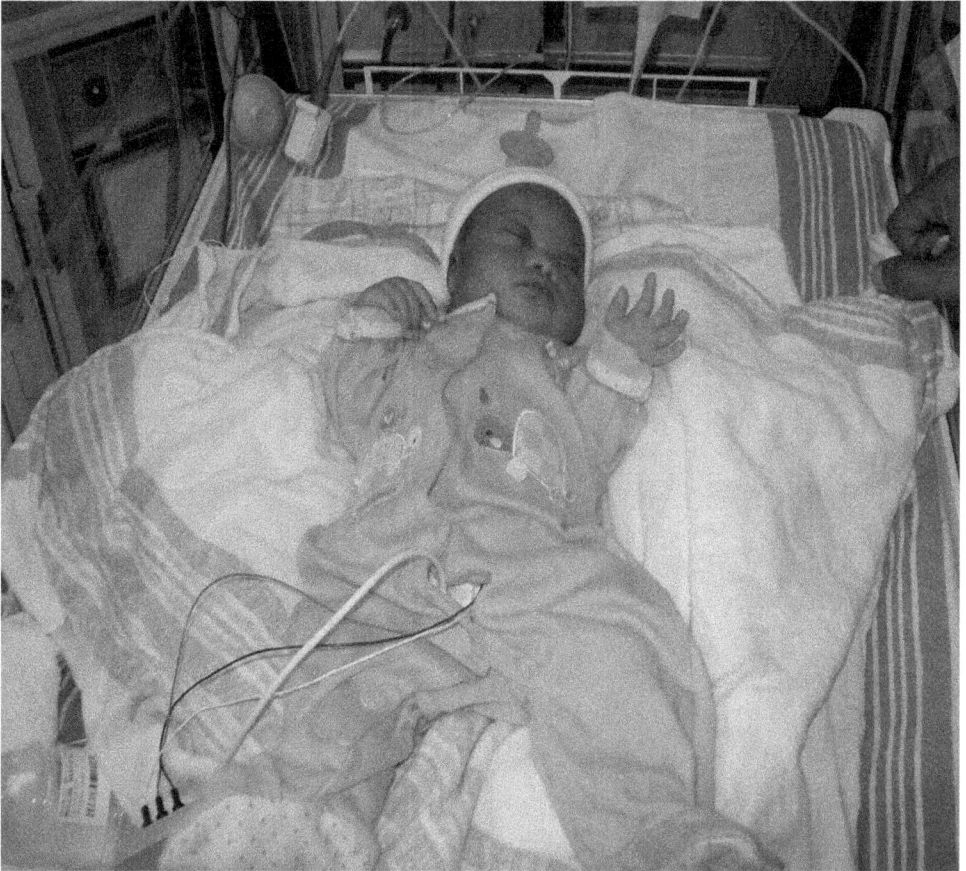

Miracle breathes on her own for the first time.

Chapter 6

Life at Home

The first months at home were truly amazing. There were moments of intense heartache and confusion. There were also moments when I was truly astonished by the work that God was doing in me and in baby Miracle.

Those were disjointed months and in some ways, it felt like a blur. But Miracle was astounding all of us with her resiliency and determination to fight for life.

Miracle didn't make the normal noises or cries that babies do. The only way I would know that she was wet was by the way she moved. It took two or three weeks after getting home before she would even cry. I had to be on watch at all times and highly attentive to her needs. There were nights when I was delirious from being so tired. I also went 2 months in which Miracle didn't maintain eye contact because babies with Down syndrome often have a difficult time focusing visually.

Finally, when Miracle started crying, it was amazing to hear her voice. While crying is a sound that irritates some parents, my child's cry was an angelic sound to my ears because it told me that my baby needed me. It also told me that there was something that she needed and that she was crying for my attention. And because of who she is, it was more special because I knew that she was fighting even to have the ability to cry out. It was like what the psalmist said:

The righteous cry out, and the LORD hears,
And delivers them out of all their troubles.

Psalms 34:17

I learned that I needed to practice Miracle's mouth closing technique through the use of a special spoon. Like I said before, children with Down's experience a lot of distress because of issues with their mouths. It is hard for them to form the necessary lip and mouth positions because of low muscle tone and delayed development. In addition, Miracle's neck was not strong enough to hold her head up. She had to learn to use the muscles in her neck as they developed and strengthened over time.

Even with all of these trials and obstacles, God still showed me that He alone is faithful. One night at Bible study, Miracle made direct eye contact with me for the first time. I was overwhelmed with joy at that moment knowing that my baby knew that her mother was there. Milestones like this are what kept me going when I sometimes thought all was lost.

This was also largely due to the support of my family and of my church. When the kids saw that Miracle had special challenges ahead of her, they began to research ways to help me out. They were frequently on the Internet looking for new ways to engage her in therapy and they began helping me out around the house so that I could give Miracle the attention she needed.

Everyone in the house began to educate themselves. Early intervention, a part of the state programming for children with disabilities, came very early and helped our family give Miracle the support she needed. The children performed their own impromptu therapy in the evenings based on what they learned in Miracle's sessions. Miracle attended the Bell Center as well as the state's Early Intervention program. Mrs. Bell and the Bell Center were also closely involved and maintained contact with Miracle for a long time. It was a blessing to see so many people eager to help Miracle along her way.

The entire family came closer to God through these interactions together and with Miracle. We as a family developed a deeper appreciation for children with special needs. We were all able to see the mighty hand of God at work and feel the presence of God in Miracle and in our family. The children were old enough to understand that Miracle had Down syndrome and they immediately changed and became so attentive to their sister and to each other. Instead of arguing, they were more apt to find common solutions and be a united front for their new sibling.

It was in the fourth month when we found out that Miracle was cleared from having any heart defects. Many children with Down syndrome have ongoing testing due to various health issues including heart problems. Fortunately, and by the grace of God, Miracle did not. She developed quickly and was a picture of health. Miracle's weight was also on target and she was able to focus and concentrate earlier than other children with her diagnosis .We were released from her routine heart doctor's care during the fourth month and it was a blessing to be able to say that God was doing miraculous things in this child's life.

Some of the other things that were amazing in Miracle's development were her confidence in walking. She walked earlier than expected and showed obvious signs of not wanting to be defined by her diagnosis.

Miracle also did not get sick a single time during her entire first year. All of my other children were in an out of the doctor's office with all of the routine ailments of childhood. Not a cold, an ear infection or a sneeze beset Miracle until she was almost one and a half years old. This is practically unheard of in Down syndrome babies and was another of the many miracles of God.

During these months, I truly believed God. In the hospital, the very words that made up Miracle's diagnosis gave me chills and brought tears to my eyes. But by the time I got home, I wasn't focused on the pain of the diagnosis; I was focused on the miracles that God was performing in Miracle's life. It was as if all of the amazing things that God was doing for Miracle were also a lesson for me. They showed me that He was still faithful, that He was an on time God, that He cared about the little things in my life and that He was a restorer of broken things. The milestones in Miracles life gave me renewed hope for tomorrow and they pushed me in the direction of a strong, lasting, committed faith in

God. It was as if all of this was meant to bring me closer to Him.

It was at this time that Romans 8:28 began to ring so true in my life.

And we know that all things work together for good to them that love God, to them who are the called according to his purpose.

All things: I began to realize that to be called according to the purpose of God was what was most important. And at this time, my purpose in Him was to be grounded and rooted in faith in Him and to the commitment to my child. And because I was called according to this purpose, ALL THINGS were going to work together for my good because I LOVED GOD.

I loved God so much that I was willing to trust Him with the life of my miracle child. I was willing to believe in the positive purpose He had for me. I was willing to go through the pain of being dealt this blow of having a child with Down syndrome and then giving her back to Him to love and nurture and treasure.

I was grateful for Miracle's awesome development. For that, to God be the Glory for no one else could have done this. The doctors and the nursing staff were amazed at what they were beginning to see. Our prayers for Miracle were being answered right before our eyes. The dim outlook that had been presented to us was beginning to diminish and our hope was coming alive. But more than that, I was grateful for God's supernatural work in my heart. He was healing dry places, renewing dry bones and bringing a well of fresh, living water to a dead and dusty soul. I felt like a revival had begun to take place on the inside of me. I was beginning to understand clearly what Isaiah 40:31 means. *"But they that wait upon the LORD shall renew their strength; they shall mount up with wings as eagles; they shall run, and not be weary; and they shall walk, and not faint"*. Not only was my physical strength being renewed but my mental strength was being renewed as well.

Chapter 7

Don't Walk in Fear

One of the hardest trials I've had to face with Miracle at home was learning to deal with my own fear.

I stated previously that when we met with Ms. Bell at the Bell Center, she looked me square in the eyes and told me that the only limits Miracle would have would be the limits that I put on her. I did not know how true this was until life with Miracle really began.

When Miracle came home, she had very low muscle tone. This meant that she was unable to hold her head up or use her muscles the way that other babies could. She had very limp legs and it took her a long time to strengthen them. It took Miracle a long time to crawl, walk and even hold her own spoon. Whenever she was required to use her muscles, she would cry because they were so under developed. Her torso was weak and we had to teach her to use the muscles in her stomach in order to keep herself sitting up or to reach for an object.

Because of this, she required extensive therapy. Therapists came to the house and taught us how to help her do the things she needed to do. There were times when the therapist would be working with Miracle and they would allow her cry which encouraging her to use her neck muscles to sit up. All of this work was for her legs and arms and even her neck. We were spending so much time learning to be therapists and rehab specialists to Miracle; it was as if we were rubbing life into her limbs.

For example, there was a time when Miracle would sit on the floor and her legs would be almost in a complete split. She would then lie in the middle of her legs, not wanting to use the strength that it took to sit up on her own. She wanted someone to pick her up and place her in a seated position. Her therapist however would leave her in that position and encourage her get up on her own. She would repeat "Miracle, you've got to get up on your own" over and over again, encouraging Miracle to do for herself what she wanted others to do for her. Nevertheless, she would just lie there and cry and cry and cry. I would be sitting next to the therapist myself, crying and sobbing because I wanted to rescue my child.

This was very hard for me. As a mother, when you hear your child cry, your natural reaction is to save them and keep them away from what is upsetting them. I wanted to rescue my child and hold her and do for her what she needed. It took everything within me not to stop the process. I knew that her therapists were doing what was best for her but it was a challenge to let them do their job.

What I had to learn was that what was happening to Miracle was not to hurt her, but to help her. She had to be placed in uncomfortable situations if she was ever going to learn to do for herself. The therapists would tell me over and over to "trust the process" and to remember that what was happening to Miracle was necessary. If I held her every time she cried, she would have never learned to strengthen her muscles. I had to make up in my mind that what was happening to Miracle was for her good.

Through the times where the family and I had to let Miracle go through this process, we learned to appreciate life. We realized that everything wasn't automatic. We take for granted that a baby will learn to sit up and roll over and do the things that a healthy, functioning child does. We were training Miracle to live, walk and move. It was a daily process that amazed us at every turn.

I want to make it known that faith in God and not being afraid of the process was what got us through this very hard time of training Miracle. I have dealt with so many parents of children with Down syndrome who are afraid to push their child to their limits. They are afraid of hurting them or making them uncomfortable. They don't want push or train them because of the fear that is holding them in place. I want the parents to know that the process is not going to hurt their child but accelerate them to the point where they need to be. It is training that strengthens and motivates them to keep going. It is no different than bodybuilding; an athlete has to train and push through their pain. Down syndrome babies have to do the same thing and push through the pain.

Eventually, we stopped treating Miracle like a fragile child. She is a normal child who with training can do all of the things that the average child can do. A parent walking in fear will hinder the growth and potential of their child. They will limit what a child with Down syndrome can do and with that kind of fear in their life, they will never reach their full potential. I did not want that for Miracle. So I became determined to not let my fear dictate how far Miracle could go. God has not given us a spirit of fear, but of power and of love and of a sound mind.

Fear has two meanings: "Forget everything and run" or "Face everything and rise." We chose to face our obstacles and allow Miracle to rise.

There is a spiritual lesson here that I think is necessary for every parent who has a child with Down. It is a lesson that extends to every believer in any situation but especially for the parent of the Down syndrome baby.

Do not walk in fear. Trust God for the process. His process is meant to help you, not harm you.

Chapter 8

The Miracle Mullen Downs Foundation

Dear Reader,

As a mother of a child with Down's syndrome, I know what it means to be in need of support. I, nor Miracle, would be where we are today without the loving support and encouragement of my husband and Miracle's father, Greg Mullen. That is why this chapter belongs to him, from his heart to yours.

Rosie

As Miracle's father, I have had the privilege of being there for Rosie and Miracle every step of the way, seeing how they have grown and found encouragement in the Lord. I want to share with you part of my journey as their main cheerleader and companion.

When Rosie and Miracle were in the hospital, the Lord spoke very clearly to me about one of the roles that I was to play in their lives. Now, being a father to Miracle and husband to Rosie was a given; I have always known that my first place is to lead and guide and protect them both. As Miracle's diagnosis came to light, I came to understand the specific challenges that both she and our family would face. I began to understand that my role was broader than what I had expected.

During the pregnancy, I began to feel in my spirit that Miracle would be born with Down syndrome. Without saying a word to Rosie, I did all the things that I was taught to do. I prayed, I rebuked, I named, I claimed, I laid hands on Rosie's stomach and cried out to God. When Miracle was born with Down syndrome, I asked the Lord why.

The Lord spoke these words to me:

"Greg, when I don't give you what you want, it is because I have a better plan for you."

I love Miracle very much and will always support her. But I would be lying if I said that I did not pray that she did not have Down syndrome when she was born. No parent would wish that for their child. So yes, for her to be free from this diagnosis was a prayer that I hoped and wished the Lord would have answered with a resounding yes.

However, when the Lord spoke these words, I knew that this diagnosis and this life were allowed by God for a reason. I believe that the Lord wanted to get glory out of our lives through a situation like this. I knew this was the reason He had spoken this. I knew that there was glory on the other side of it. When I came to the realization that there was meaning and purpose in it all, I was determined to allow God's glory to reign in this situation.

That is why I founded the Miracle Mullen Downs Foundation.

The mission of the Miracle Mullen Downs Foundation is to help educate and provide training for families affected by Down syndrome. Our goal is to ensure that children with Down syndrome get help early and often because the sooner they are in therapy and seeing the necessary physicians, the better their chances are for living a productive life. We endeavor to provide families with information and support.

The Lord showed me this very clearly. When He spoke, it was as if He was charging Rosie to be Miracle's primary support in the household as mother and nurturer and me to be her protector in the world, the one to make her story mean something to others.

The vision that God gave me over time with the foundation was to:

- Change the lives of families affected by Down syndrome by giving them hope through training assistance.
- Educate parents and siblings on how to adjust to this new lifestyle and teach them what to do to help their miracle child to excel.
- See that children with Down syndrome get the best possible care.
- Ensure that no Miracle child is left behind due to their condition.

Miracle and I have been on television, radio and have done numerous speaking engagements about the effects of Down syndrome on a child and on a family. We have traveled the country and have been able to speak into the lives of many families, offering them hope, encouragement, information and love. We have done more than I could have ever possibly dreamed of. It was all because the Lord said that He had something better in store.

The reason we do this is not for fame or for fortune. If we were seeking to get rich from this, it would never happen. We do this because we as a family, understand the necessity of finding support, encouragement and hope in the midst of a diagnosis that seems tragic. We know what it is like to need help.

Now that the Lord has given us help and comfort through so many wonderful, supportive people, we offer the same help and comfort that we have been given. It is the epitome of what the scriptures call us to do:

Blessed be the God and Father of our Lord Jesus Christ, the Father of mercies and God of all comfort, 4 who comforts us in all our tribulation that we may be able to comfort those who are in any trouble, with the comfort with which we ourselves are comforted by God.

2 Corinthians 1:3, 4

Two years after the Miracle Mullen Downs Foundation, we also founded the Miracle Sisters. The Miracle Sisters are Miracles three older siblings who are singing to bringing glory to God and awareness to Down syndrome. Their first CD was released July 27th 2014 titled "He Knows Me". This title was derived from the fact that God not only knows Miracle, but He also knew what we were experiencing. It is a Jeremiah 29:11 experience.

We also started the Miracle Center in August of 2013. This center exists to train babies with Down syndrome and other special needs. It gives them one on one training and attention. Miracle was able to attend her own center and graduate from there as well.

My encouragement to those families that are supporting a child with Down syndrome is this: Love your child. Place no limits on them. When you are in need of encouragement, reach out to those around you. Search out places like the Miracle Mullen Downs Foundation or other local places in your area. Look to the resource page of this book for help.

More than anything else you should reach out to God, knowing that when He doesn't give you what you asked for, it is because He has a better plan. God gives special children to special people.

In Love,

Greg Mullen

Chapter 9

LOVE

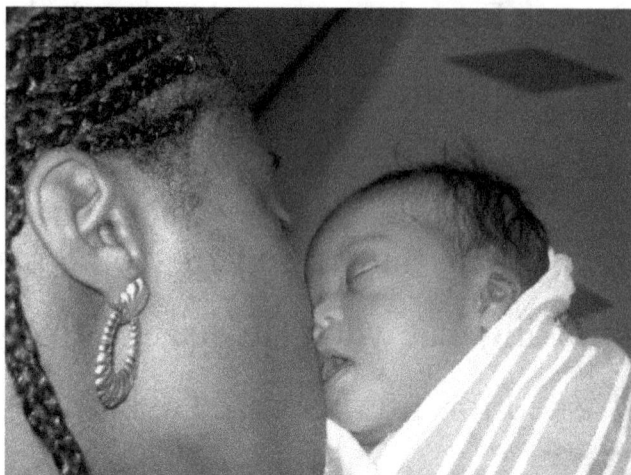

For God so loved the world, that he gave his only begotten Son, that whosoever believeth in him should not perish, but have everlasting life.

John 3:16

As we come to the end of my story, I want to leave you with something that is at the heart of my miracle story.

When Jesus Christ died on the cross, He did a mighty work in and for us. He looked beyond every shortcoming and downfall that we had as sinners and still gave up His life on our behalf. He allowed us second, third and fourth chances to live and have an abundant life.

John 3:16 say's that because God loved us, He gave up His Son to die for us. He left us an example of what true love is. True love equals sacrifice. True love equals giving.

You must be a giver, just as Jesus gave. Because man was so lost and alone, dying in sin, God had to really and truly show us genuine love. Even in all of our shortcomings, the Father still sent his Son Jesus to woo and romance man back to Himself. By Him giving and doing this awesome work for us, He set an example that we should follow; an example that says we should give love to those who are in need.

Jesus loved so he gave.

If you love your special needs child, you too have to give.

If you truly want your miracle child's life to be abundant, healthy and full of limitless potential, the love you have for them must supercede anything else. You must give your love and devotion to them wholeheartedly.

You must love them so much that you are able to walk with them through their growth. You must be ready to show the same love to others that God has shown us; that is true love. This kind of love sometimes calls for sacrificial giving. You must be willing to give of your time, talent, treasure and energy to the betterment of your miracle child. You must be willing to go great lengths to provide and protect them, to nurture them and show them affection.

Embrace your miracle child. It is all about what is on the inside of you that will be poured into them. Your love for them must be limitless. With this level of love, they can grow to their full capacity, knowing that someone loves them.

Your love for them supersedes all else in their lives.

God loved you. God loves you. You have to give the same to your miracle child. You must be a giver. The word of God speaks about the fact that it is better to give than to receive and selfishness will only limit how far your miracle child can go.

Some people, out of their selfishness, give up their special needs child; they abandon them because they believe that the children are a burden or unworthy of affection. They might even believe that the job of caring for them is too large for them to handle. I am here to tell you that those children can indeed be kept and loved like any other child. They too can give and receive love.

You have been given a special child for a special reason. If God gave them to you, He will give you the means to accomplish this task. God gives you this promise in the book of Philippians:

Being confident of this very thing, that he which hath begun a good work in you will perform it until the day of Jesus Christ:

Philippians 1:6

I wrote this story so that you would know that God can get glory out of your life and the life of your miracle child. You can be at peace and still be able to give this love to your child. It all comes down to your perspective: You can either look at the situation negatively or you can believe that your miracle child is a blessing from God.

Loving your miracle child will require time, finances and energy. This is something that you must be prepared to give. But regardless of all of that, you must know that God is a keeper of your soul and He shall provide. He will supply everything needed to accomplish your task. Do not feel that this is something that you can not conquer. Walk in love and know that you have an opportunity to give and operate in the love of God.

They can grow into wonderful men and women of God if you allow the miracle of God to manifest in your house. I would challenge you to believe God for all that He can do in their lives. Trust in Him, obey His word and show His love. Be the vehicle that He uses to minister to your miracle and believe me, you will find that you are blessed.

Thank you for taking the time to read about my miracle child and all the things that God has done in my life. I pray that you have been blessed and that you are encouraged to embrace the miracles of God in your own life.

The Lord bless you and keep you;

The Lord make His face shine upon you, And be gracious to you;

The Lord lift up His countenance upon you, And give you peace." '

Numbers 6:24-26

Blessings to you and a life full of miracles,

Rosie & Miracle Mullen

Appendix I

Resources

It is our prayer that if you are the parent or family member of a child with Down's syndrome, that you would be equipped with information for your journey.

If you need help, contact the local early intervention center in your state. Obtaining services as early as possible is crucial to your child's development. Below are some other resources available to you.

Miracle Mullen Downs Foundation:

www.miraclemullendownsfoundation.org

National Down syndrome Society

666 Broadway, 8th Floor
New York New York 10012
(800) 221-4602
http://www.ndss.org/

Global Down syndrome Foundation

The Global Down Syndrome Foundation's primary focus is to support the Linda Crnic Institute for Down Syndrome, headquartered at the University of Colorado School of Medicine on the Anschutz Medical Campus in Aurora, CO. It is the first academic home in the United States committed solely to research and medical care for people with Down syndrome.
www.globaldownsyndrome.org

Downs Designs: **Karen Bowersox**

karen@downsdesigns.com
8796 Tyler Boulevard
Mentor, Oh 44060
440) 290-8903
www.downsdesigns.com

Appendix II
Down syndrome Explained
What is Down syndrome?

Down syndrome is a genetic condition that is characterized by typical features. It is caused by an abnormality in the genetic material and it affects all races and all economic groups equally.

Why do they think that our baby has Down syndrome?

Babies with Down syndrome do look slightly different from other babies and therefore they can usually be identified at birth. Some of the typical features include:

- eyes that slant upwards;

- tiny folds covering the inner corners of the eyes (epicanthic folds);
- small white flecks on the iris (Brushfield spots)
- a small nose with a broad, flat bridge;
- a small mouth which makes the tongue appear large
- small low set ears;
- a single crease on the palm of the hand;
- short hands and fingers;
- inclining pinkie
- wider gap between the big toe and second toe
- A slightly flattened appearance of the back of the head.

Other Features

- Unusual looseness of the joints
- Poor muscle tone (hypotonia) making the baby feel and appear "floppy"
- Loose skin folds at the back of the neck

- Heart defects occur in about 50% of cases
- Eye defects occur in 60% of cases
- Hearing defects may occur and can affect speech and language
- Developmental delay (intellectual disability varies from mild to moderate)

Not all these traits mentioned are found in every child with Down syndrome. Like other children, children with Down syndrome resemble their parents, e.g. hair and eye color but they also have some of the typical features of Down syndrome. Furthermore each person with Down syndrome is a unique individual and can vary enormously in appearance, temperament and ability. It is also important to note that a person's appearance has nothing to do with his intellectual ability. Therefore a person, who has more of these above mentioned characteristics, is not necessarily more intellectually impaired. Down syndrome is not diagnosed only on the basis of physical characteristics; it must be confirmed by means of a chromosome analysis. This is a special type of laboratory test performed on a sample of blood from the baby. Your doctor will be able to tell you more about this test.

Where did the name "Down syndrome" come from?

Down syndrome is named after Dr. Langdon Down, the physician who first described its features in 1866. The word "syndrome" means "a collection of signs and symptoms usually found in combination.

What causes Down syndrome?

Down syndrome is caused by extra genetic material. The genetic material is present in every human body cell and is arranged in tiny structures called chromosomes. They are the building blocks, which give us our individual characteristics. For example they determine the color of our hair and our eyes and many other characteristics. Each human body cell contains 23 pairs (46) chromosomes, except the sex cells (egg cells of a woman and sperm of a man), which each contains only 23 chromosomes. Egg cells and sperm are formed by a special cell division process during which the chromosome pairs divide and only one chromosome of each pair is included in a sex cell. The egg cell and sperm therefore each receives only one copy of each chromosome pair. During fertilization a sperm of the father fuses with an egg cell of the mother. The fertilized egg cell then contains 23 pairs of chromosomes (46 in total). One chromosome of each pair comes from the father and the other one of each of the pairs from the mother. The fertilized egg cell divides rapidly in the womb and eventually the baby is formed. Each of the body cells of the baby also contains 23 pairs (46) chromosomes. When a blood sample of a baby is analyzed in a laboratory, a photograph of the chromosomes is taken under a microscope. The chromosomes on the photo are then cut out, numbered and arranged according to pairs. Such a chromosome arrangement is called a karyotype. Note that the chromosomes are arranged and numbered according to a specific pattern, namely from large to small. One of the smallest chromosomes is numbered as number 21. It is the chromosome number 21 that is involved in the origin of Down syndrome.

It is important to understand that Down syndrome is not caused by anything the mother or father did or failed to do during the pregnancy.

There are different types of Down syndrome:

- **<u>Trisomy 21 type of Down syndrome</u>** Trisomy 21 is the most common type of Down syndrome and is the cause of approximately 90-95% of all cases of Down syndrome. Trisomy type of Down syndrome is not hereditary! In young mothers the chance of a second baby being born with Down syndrome is therefore very small. Trisomy 21 (also known as non-disjunction type) occurs when the two number 21 chromosomes fail to separate and both instead of one, become incorporated into either the egg cell or the sperm. This cell then has 24 chromosomes instead of the normal 23. This phenomenon of the chromosome not separating is called non-disjunction. With fertilization, the sex cell of one of the parents (egg cell or sperm) with the two number 21 chromosomes (and therefore 24 chromosomes in total), fuses with the normal sex cell of the other parent (egg cell or sperm with 23 chromosomes) to form a fertilized egg cell with 47 chromosomes. When this fertilized cell starts to divide, it eventually develops into a baby who has an extra number 21 chromosome in each body cell and hence Down Syndrome. Trisomy 21 may be caused by non-disjunction during the formation of either the egg cells of the mother or the sperm of the father. The chances of Trisomy 21 however seem to be increased in women in their late thirties and older.

- **The mosaic type of Down syndrome** This type of Down syndrome is very rare, not hereditary and the chance of a second baby born with it is small. Mosaic type is also known as Mosaic-ism. This is caused by non-disjunction of the chromosome **pair** number

21 **shortly after fertilization**. The cells of the person with this type of Down syndrome have a mosaic pattern. The result is that some cells contain an extra chromosome number 21 (and therefore 47 chromosomes) while the other cells contain only 46 chromosomes (the normal number). Such a baby may only show partial features of the condition. Some of these babies look less affected than other babies with Down syndrome, but not all of them do.

- **<u>The trans-location type of Down syndrome</u>** A baby sometimes has all the clinical symptoms of Down syndrome but only 46 chromosomes in every cell. With Trans-location, the baby has a normal number of chromosomes but extra chromosomal material. In these cases it is found that, over and above a normal pair number 21, these babies also have an extra part of a chromosome number 21, attached to another chromosome, which usually is chromosome number 14. This is called trans-location type of Down syndrome. This type of Down syndrome **can be hereditary**! Either parent can carry a trans-location without showing any symptoms. In this case the risk to have another child with this type of Down syndrome for the parents concerned, or for other members of the family, can be quite high. It is strongly advised that a chromosome test is done on both parents and that they seek genetic counseling if they plan further pregnancies. It is important to remember that the type of Down syndrome that is diagnosed makes no difference to the eventual development and potential of the child.

• **Why did this happen to us?** Down syndrome can occur in any marriage, to people of all races and religions. It is not caused by food or medicine taken or by any other event e.g. an accident during pregnancy. Neither of the parents is to blame and therefore you have no cause to feel guilty or blame your spouse. Try not to listen to superstitions and unlikely explanations given by well intentioned people.

References

national down syndrome society

http://www.ndss.org/index.php?option=com_content&view=article&id=54&Itemid=74

About Down Syndrome

http://www.monicaanddavid.com/

http://www.monicaanddavid.com/learn-more/about-down-syndrome/

http://health.nytimes.com/health/guides/disease/down-syndrome/overview.html

About the Author

Rosie Mullen was born July 4th 1966, in Gainesville, AL, the fourth child of P. S. and Christine Jenkins. She is a 1984 graduate of Livingston High School in Livingston, AL. She was married to Gregory K. Mullen in July of 1985 and they have five children. They have been married for nearly thirty years. Rosie grew up knowing that something was different about her but just could not pinpoint what it was until in 1997 when she heard the Voice of God tell her she had been chosen for a special purpose. She was licensed to preach by Bishop Earnest L. Palmer at the Cornerstone Full Gospel Baptist Church in 1998 and Ordained by Pastor Gregory K. Mullen and The Fairview Baptist Church in 2002.

Rosie is a giver, a lover of life and family, a wife, a mother and a prophetic woman of God. God has given her a strong compassion for hurting women, to the point that she can feel their pain. She did volunteer work with Jessie's Place and The Lovelady Center, both of which are homes for women and children.

Rosie is a graduate of Miles College with a B. S. Degree in Business Administration. She received her MBA in Accounting and Human Resources from Argosy University. She spent fifteen years in secular employment but has now taken the leap of faith to become the Chief Financial Officer with a Transitional Facility. She has done theological studies at Birmingham Baptist Bible College.

God has also allowed her to write two books "Breaking Free" and "Walking in The Spirit" a guide to quit smoking.

www.ingramcontent.com/pod-product-compliance
Lightning Source LLC
Chambersburg PA
CBHW062004040426
42447CB00010B/1896